FUN-FILLED
5- to 10-MINUTE
MATH ACTIVITIES FOR
YOUNG LEARNERS

200 Instant Kid-Pleasing Activities That Build Essential Early Math Skills for Circle Time, Transition Time—or Any Time!

by Deborah Diffily

S C H O L A S T I C
PROFESSIONAL BOOKS

NEW YORK   TORONTO   LONDON   ~DNEY
MEXICO CITY   NEW DELHI   HONG KO~   ~UENOS AIRES

Acknowledgment

Thank you to the children of Trinity Lutheran Child Care Center and Riverside and Alice Carlson Applied Learning Centers for sharing their math moments.

Cover design by Solás
Illustrations by Cary Pillo
Interior design by Josué Castilleja
Interior photographs by Mike Hawkins

ISBN 0-439-31890-4

TABLE OF CONTENTS

About This Book 5

Math Skills and Concepts

    One-to-One Correspondence 6

    Counting 11

    Number Sense 16

    Comparing Quantities 18

    Adding 21

    Subtracting 26

    Wholes and Parts/Fractions 30

    Introduction to Multiplying/Dividing 32

    Geometry 34

    Measuring 40

    Estimating 44

    Time 47

    Money 50

    Graphing 52

    Patterning 57

    Sorting and Classifying 61

ABOUT THIS BOOK

Young children do not separate learning into distinct categories or content areas. Teachers may call a certain period of the day "Math Time" or refer to one area of the classroom as the math center. Children, however, do not limit their mathematical learning to particular times of the day or to certain places in the classroom. They are just as likely to count objects in the science center or to sort items during their dramatic play. Because young children are constantly learning, early childhood educators weave math skills and concepts into many of their students' daily activities.

Just as they learn throughout the day, all children learn in different ways. They do not all learn the same skill or concept through the same activity, and they rarely learn a skill the first time they are introduced to it. Young children typically need many experiences with a single concept before they develop an accurate understanding of it. Children learn concepts more easily and remember them for longer periods of time when the activities they are involved in are meaningful.

Because not all activities are equally meaningful to individual children, early childhood educators offer different ways to interact with the same concept. While skills and concepts can and should be taught during designated math times, it is more effective for young children when math concepts are also reinforced at other times during the day.

In this book, you will find activities that can be incorporated into circle time as a whole-group exercise, into center time with small groups or individual students, into transitional time, and during read-alouds using extension activities related to the books. The activities are labeled with the initials W, S, I, T, or RA to suggest the setting for each activity.

The ideas presented in this book are not meant to take the place of designated times when the whole class is focused on mathematics, but to offer ways to supplement regular math instruction. The activities have therefore been sorted according to the math skills they reinforce. We hope you enjoy the book!

ONE-TO-ONE CORRESPONDENCE

W Whole-group activity   **S** Small-group activity

I Individual activity   **T** Transition   **RA** Read-aloud

W How Many Noses? How Many Chins?

Touch the nose of each child gathered for circle time and lead the counting, "One...two...three..." and so on until all children have been counted. Then point to the name of each child posted in a pocket chart or on the wall near the meeting area. Again, invite the group to chant, "One...two...three" until all names have been counted. Both numbers should be the same—one nose for each name. Repeat the activity counting chins, heads, and so on.

S Find the Pair

Put socks in the middle of the circle of children. Make sure you have enough pairs so that each child in the group can find a match. Invite children to sift through the socks, find pairs, and fold them together.

> **Teaching Tip #1**
> After the "Find the Pair" activity, unfold the socks and put them in a laundry basket. Put the basket in the home center and encourage children to match the socks during self-selected center time.

S Find a Friend

Reinforce one-to-one correspondence by asking each child to find one person to work with as a partner during different activities. The partners can read a book together, play short math games, share a favorite part of a book, or read their writings to each other.

(S) Find the Props for "The Three Little Bears"

Organize a small group of children to locate props in the classroom to dramatize "The Three Little Bears." They will need to find three bowls, three spoons, three chairs, and three beds. In addition to enhancing the concept of one-to-one correspondence, this activity will also help children understand the concept of small, medium, and large. With a little imagination and brain-storming from the class, the group can be asked to locate additional props, such as three combs, three toothbrushes, or three pairs of socks.

(S) Bowls and Spoons

Ask a pair of children to prepare the class' snacks by unstacking bowls and putting a plastic spoon in each bowl. Make sure that there are enough bowls for everyone.

(S) Setting the Table

Encourage children to set a plate, glass, napkin, and flatware on the home center's table for the children who are playing in the home center. You may also want to draw the place setting on plastic place mats and ask children to match the actual plate, glass, napkin, and flatware to those drawn on the place mat.

(I) Cheese and Cracker Snacks

Offer small cubes of cheese and crackers for a snack. Have children get their own snack, putting four crackers on a small paper plate, then putting one cube of cheese on each cracker. You can also do this activity using a variety of other snacks that require two items to be matched up before eating.

Ⓘ Cotton Ball Grids

Provide containers of cotton balls and card stock with large square grids. Encourage children to put a small dab of glue ("dot, dot, not a lot") in each square and place a cotton ball on each dot of glue.

Ⓘ Build a City

Provide a child with a die, interlocking cubes, a copy of My City Game Mat (page 10), and a crayon. Have the child roll the die 10 times. Each time he rolls the die, he counts the dots on the die, connects that many cubes, then places the cubes vertically on one of the squares on the game mat. Have the child record the numeral on the square to show how many stories high the building is.

Ⓣ Marching Mates

Have each child find a partner. Ask children to link arms and march around the classroom to the beat of John Phillip Sousa or similar marching music.

Ⓣ Action Rhyme

As children gather for circle time, begin to recite this rhyme accompanied by the obvious actions:

Feet and Hands

Two little feet go jump, jump, jump,
Two little hands go thump, thump, thump,
One little body turns round and round.
One little child sits quietly down.
Two little feet go tap, tap, tap,
Two little hands go clap, clap, clap.
A quick little leap up from the chair.
Two little arms reach high in the air.

T Chant

To refocus children's attention during circle time, begin to recite this rhyme and they will join in:

Things That Go Together

A foot goes with a sock.
A key goes with a lock.
A tick goes with a tock.
And chopsticks with a wok.

A queen goes with a king.
A plane goes with a wing.
A bong goes with a bing.
And a finger with a ring.

Invite the class to create additional verses.

RA Literacy Links

How Many Feet in the Bed? by Diane Johnston Hamm (Simon & Schuster, 1994). This simple counting book counts by twos as a little girl climbs into her parents' bed with her father—two people make four feet. As other family members join them, the total number of feet in the bed reaches 10. As each family member climbs out of bed, they count down to no feet in the bed.

Try This! Invite children to form a large circle and put a sheet in the middle of the circle. As you read the book aloud a second time, point to certain children to play the characters getting into and out of bed. Have another child hold signs labeled 2, 4, 6, 8, and 10, and show the card that matches the number of feet in the bed at each point during the story.

Try This, Too! Ask children to sketch the family getting into and out of bed. Assist the children in posting the drawings in sequential order of 2 feet, 4 feet, 6 feet, 8 feet, 10 feet, 8 feet, 6 feet, 4 feet, 2 feet, and 0 feet.

The M&Ms Brand Counting Book by Barbara Barbieri McGrath (Charlesbridge, 1994). Use the pictures of colorful candies and rhyming phrases at the beginning of the book to teach the numbers 1 through 12. Following the counting portion of the book, the concepts of sets, shapes, and subtraction are introduced.

Try This! Reproduce the counting pages of the book and provide children with M&Ms to place on the pages.

My City Game Mat

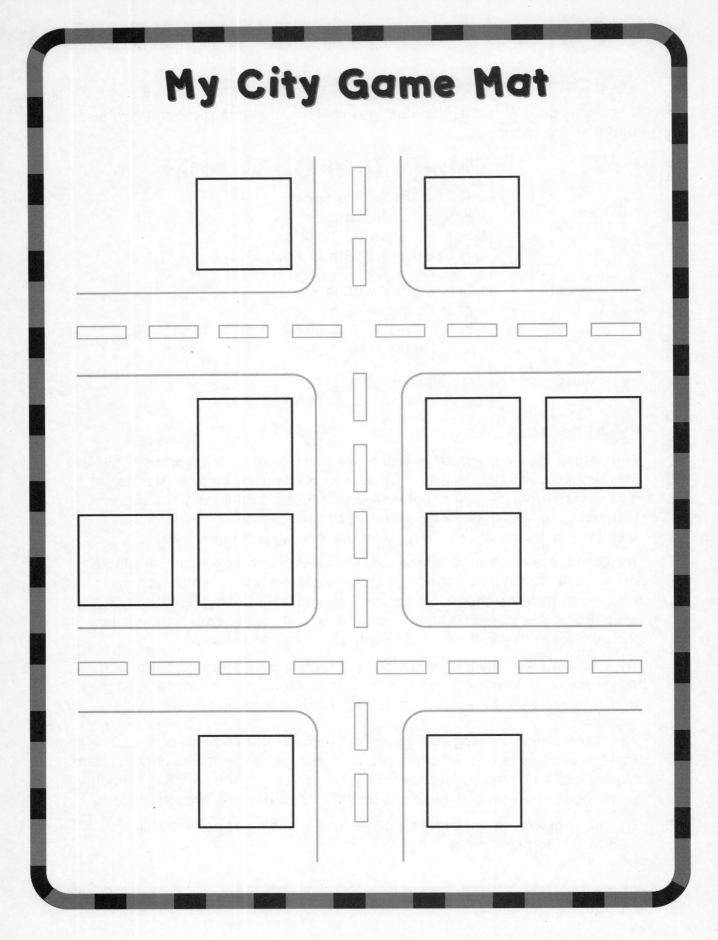

FUN-FILLED 5-TO-10-MINUTE MATH ACTIVITIES FOR YOUNG LEARNERS

COUNTING

Ⓦ Whole-group activity Ⓢ Small-group activity
Ⓘ Individual activity Ⓣ Transition ㏚ Read-aloud

Ⓦ Taking Attendance

As children enter the classroom in the morning, have each child move his or her name card from the "I am at home" column to the "I am at school" column. During circle time, count together the number of children who are at school and the number of children who are at home. Write the numbers representing each group on chart paper.

Ⓦ Counting the Days in School

Put a large sheet of chart paper on a wall and label it with the title "How Many Days Have We Been in School?" Every day, record the number of days so far in the school year on the paper. You may want to use different colored numbers for the 5s and 10s to teach skip counting.

How Many Days Have We Been in School?

1	2	3	4	5	6	7	8	9	10
11	12	13	14	15	16	17	18	19	20
21	22								

Ⓦ Counting the Days Until . . .

Mark special days such as birthdays or holidays on the class calendar. Display a sign reading "_____ days until _____" beside the calendar. Change the number every day as you get closer to the special day. This offers children a lesson on how to count backwards, as well as another reason to count something meaningful to them.

(S) Taking Inventory

Create inventory cards to help keep track of supplies in different learning centers (for example, bottles of glue in the art center, poetry books in the reading center, colored pencils in the writing center, and so on). Pair up children and ask each pair to pick an inventory card. Have them count the items listed on their card and report missing items to you so that they can be replaced. (Note: You can also use this activity to teach comparing quantities.)

(I) Step Counting

Cut out child-size footprints from felt, card stock, or similar material. Number the footprints and place them on the floor. You can have the footprints lead from one center to another, or just have them go anywhere. Encourage children to count as they follow the footprints.

(I) Counting Books

Offer children several sheets of self-adhesive colored dots and blank books. Encourage children to make their own counting books by writing a number on each page and attaching the same number of dots.

Teaching Tip #2
To make a blank counting book, fold three 8 1/2- by 11-inch sheets of paper in half. Staple the spine with an extra-long stapler.

(I) Lunch Count

Ask a volunteer to announce the menu choices for lunch. Invite children to stand, indicating their lunch choice. Then have your volunteer write the number of children on the lunch count form.

I Collections

Start a class collection of a popular item (seashells, rocks, leaves, or anything else that interests children) and add to the collection regularly. Keep index cards and pencils next to the collection. Challenge children to count the collection every few days and post the total number of items on a card. Remind them to write the date on the card as well.

Teaching Tip #3

Young children love to collect things, and they are much more inclined to count things that are important to them. For children who need extra experience in counting, find items that they particularly like. Start collections in different centers or areas of the classroom. For example, the class can collect nuts and bolts in the block center, cookie cutters in the home center, seashells in the science center, measuring cups in the water center, and so on.

T Action Rhyme

As children gather for circle time, recite this rhyme accompanied by actions:

One, Two, Buckle My Shoe

One, two,
Buckle my shoe.
Three, four,
Shut the door.
Five, six,
Pick up sticks.
Seven, eight,
Lay them straight.
Nine, ten,
Do it again!

T **Chant**

Five minutes before lunch time—or while the class is waiting for their turn at the gym or library—begin this chant:

The Ants Go Marching

The ants go marching one by one, hurrah, hurrah!
The ants go marching one by one, hurrah, hurrah!
The ants go marching one by one,
The little one stops to suck his thumb
And they all go marching down to the ground
To get out of the rain, BOOM! BOOM! BOOM!

The ants go marching two by two, hurrah, hurrah!
The ants go marching two by two, hurrah, hurrah!
The ants go marching two by two,
The little one stops to tie his shoe
And they all go marching down to the ground
To get out of the rain, BOOM! BOOM! BOOM!

The ants go marching three by three, hurrah, hurrah . . .
The little one stops to climb a tree. . . .

The ants go marching four by four, hurrah, hurrah . . .
The little one stops to shut the door. . . .

The ants go marching five by five, hurrah, hurrah . . .
The little one stops to take a dive. . . .

The ants go marching six by six, hurrah, hurrah . . .
The little one stops to pick up sticks. . . .

The ants go marching seven by seven, hurrah, hurrah . . .
The little one stops to pray to heaven. . . .

The ants go marching eight by eight, hurrah, hurrah . . .
The little one stops to shut the gate. . . .

The ants go marching nine by nine, hurrah, hurrah . . .
The little one stops to check the time. . . .

The ants go marching ten by ten, hurrah, hurrah!
The ants go marching ten by ten, hurrah, hurrah!
The ants go marching ten by ten,
The little one stops to say "THE END"
And they all go marching down to the ground
To get out of the rain, BOOM! BOOM! BOOM!

Teaching Tip #4

Put small plastic ants in the math or science center.
Challenge children to arrange the ants in different arrays,
marching two by two, three by three, and so on.

RA Literacy Links

Let's Count by Tana Hoban (Greenwillow, 1999).
Huge numerals with number words fill one page, while the facing page features a photograph with a corresponding number of everyday objects (one chicken, two ice-cream cones, 50 eggs, 100 spools of thread).

Try This! Create pages for a class-made book called "Let's Count Stickers." Modeling for the class, write the numeral "1" and put one sticker on the page. Open the rings and add this page between the already prepared title page and back cover. On following days, create additional pages for the book. Each day, have the class choral read the book before placing it back in the reading center.

Try This, Too! Place blank books, markers, and stickers in the writing center or the math center so that children can create their own copies of "Let's Count Stickers."

Spunky Monkeys on Parade by Stuart J. Murphy (HarperTrophy, 1999).
Skip counting is encouraged in this book as children count the monkeys who are riding bicycles in pairs, cartwheeling in groups of three, and marching in groups of four.

Try This! Have children dramatize the action in the book and chant the skip counting.

NUMBER SENSE

W Whole-group activity **S** Small-group activity
I Individual activity **T** Transition **RA** Read-aloud

W All-Out Number Sentences

Have children brainstorm all the number combinations for any given number. Transcribe children's suggestions for number combinations in the form of number sentences. For example, combinations for 5 are 0+5, 5+0, 1+4, 4+1, 2+3, 3+2.

W Pick a Card, Any Card

Have one child select a card from a deck of playing cards (with all the face cards removed) and hold it on his or her forehead with the number facing out. Invite the child to ask his or her classmates a series of questions to determine the number. Questions might include, "Is it an even number?" or "Is it larger than 5?" and so on, until the number becomes obvious. You can modify the game so that the goal is to determine the number on the card in the fewest number of questions.

W What is 5?

Gather children in a circle. Place a blank posterboard in the middle of the circle and write the numeral 5 at the top of the posterboard. Ask children to think of ways to show 5 (e.g., with fingers on a hand, toes on a foot, petals on a flower, names with five letters, number sentences that equal 5). Give a marker to the first four children who think of a way to show 5 and have them draw their ideas. As each child finishes, ask him or her to give the marker to another child. You may want to discuss this activity over several days to give children more time to think of ways to show five.

(S) Toothpick Numbers

Model for children how to use two groups of toothpicks to represent a single number. For example, 2 toothpicks and 1 toothpick equal 3 toothpicks; or 3 toothpicks and 0 toothpicks equal 3 toothpicks.

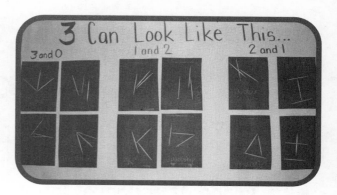

(I) Paper Clip Counting

Challenge children to write a number on an index card, count the correct number of paper clips, then slip the paper clips on the index card.

Teaching Tip #5
"Toothpick Numbers" and "Paper Clip Counting" are good activities for the math center. Children who are still developing number sense can be successful with small numbers, while children who are more advanced can choose higher numbers and be challenged at their own level of mathematical understanding.

(RA) Literacy Links

What Comes in 2's, 3's, & 4's? by Suzanne Aker (Aladdin, 1992). Focusing on the numbers in the title, this book goes beyond the typical counting book and examines familiar objects that are usually seen in pairs or in groups of 3s or 4s.

Try This! Display three posterboards labeled "2," "3," and "4." Ask children to add drawings or pictures (cut out from magazines, catalogs, newspapers, or grocery circulars) to represent items that come in that particular number. Later, you can add posterboards labeled with larger numbers.

12 Ways to Get to 11 by Eve Merriam (Aladdin, 1996). Merriam shows various combinations of objects that can be added together to reach the number 11. Objects are related in some way, but are not always obvious. For example, on one page the reader counts 11 items that come out of the magician's hat: 4 banners, 5 rabbits, 1 pitcher of water, and 1 bouquet of flowers.

Try This! Encourage children to create their own pages of 11 related objects and bind the pages into a book.

COMPARING QUANTITIES

W Whole-group activity   **S** Small-group activity
I Individual activity   **T** Transition   **RA** Read-aloud

W Taking Attendance, Too

In this extension of the counting activity "Taking Attendance" (page 11), write the number of children who are in class and the number who are not on chart paper. Compare the numbers and compute the difference.

W Voting Issues

Extend any voting activity your class does (e.g., "Voting for Read-Aloud" or "Voting for Favorite Book of the Week," page 53) by counting and comparing the number of votes for each choice.

W Comparing Candies

Have children count out 20 colored candies (e.g., Skittles or M&Ms), put them in a resealable bag, and bring them to the large-group meeting area. Ask questions that encourage children to examine their collection and compare quantities with each other. For example, "Who has the most reds?" or "Who has the fewest greens?"

S Dice Roll

Demonstrate how to play "Dice Roll" with a partner. Both players roll a die at the same time. One player announces the number on the die and makes a comparison statement such as, "My 6 is larger than your 3," or "My 2 is smaller than your 5."

S Battle

Model a similar game to "Dice Roll" using playing cards (use a deck with the aces and face cards removed). Deal the cards evenly between two players, stacking the cards face down in front of each player. Both players turn over a card at the same time and announce the number. Whoever has the larger number "wins" both cards. Play continues until one person runs out of cards.

(S) Distribution of Materials

Use the number of children in the class—whether it's 10 or 25—to compare as they count materials needed by everyone in class. Ask a pair of children to gather enough clipboards—or pencils, copies of a poem, or any other item—for everyone in the class. Encourage both children to repeatedly compare the number of items that they've gathered to the number of items that they need until both numbers are equal.

(S) Taking Inventory, Too

Extend the counting activity "Taking Inventory" (page 12) by asking children to compare the quantity listed on an inventory card to the actual number of items they count in a center. Have them report missing items to you so that they can be replaced.

(S) Permission Forms

Put a small group of children in charge of counting permission forms (e.g., for field trips) as the forms are returned to school. Each day, have the group announce the total number of forms that were sent home, the total number of forms that have been returned, and the total number that is still needed.

(I) Comparing First and Last Names

Make a copy of "How Long Is Your Name?" (page 20) for each child. Ask each child to write his or her first name in the top row of squares, the last name in the bottom row. Have each child decide whether the top name has more, less, or the same number of letters as the bottom name. Challenge children to repeat this activity using the names of other children (they can copy the spelling of names from the attendance chart or ask other children to spell their names for them).

(RA) Literacy Link

Just Enough Carrots by Stuart J. Murphy (HarperCollins, 1997).
On a grocery-shopping trip with his mother, a little rabbit compares the food in their shopping cart to the food in other shopping carts. He complains that they are not buying enough carrots and are buying too many cans of worms.

Try This! Ask children to determine how many carrots would be "just enough" for everyone in the class to have two carrots. Use any number of carrots, depending on the children's ability to work with larger numbers.

How Long Is Your Name?

Write your first name here. Put one letter in each box.

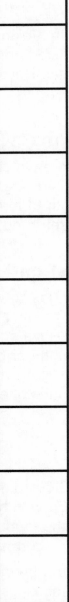

Write your last name here. Put one letter in each box.

Does one name have more letters than the other?

Which one has more letters?

FUN-FILLED 5-TO-10-MINUTE MATH ACTIVITIES FOR YOUNG LEARNERS

ADDING

W Whole-group activity **S** Small-group activity

I Individual activity **T** Transition **RA** Read-aloud

W Two-Color Counter Addition

Distribute three two-color counters to each child. Have children hold the counters in their hands about a foot above the floor and drop the counters. Ask each child to describe his or her set of counters (e.g., one red and two yellows, or two reds and one yellow) and write the equations on chart paper (e.g., 1+2 or 2+1). Point out how everyone always ends up with a total of three counters no matter how many turns up red or yellow. In the next few days, distribute four counters, then five, and so on.

Teaching Tip #6
As a follow-up to "Two-Color Counter Addition," give each child an index card and a sheet of self-adhesive red and yellow circles. Have children recreate their set of counters on their index cards. The larger the number of counters used, the more combinations will come up. Post all index cards created for one number. For example, if children are working with the number 8, the combinations would include 1+7, 7+1, 2+6, 6+2, 3+5, 5+3, 4+4.

S Double Dice Addition

Have children work in pairs, taking turns throwing two dice and adding the numbers together. At each turn, the players record their sums on a sheet of paper. Have children play for five minutes, then compare their sums to see how many times each number appears for both players.

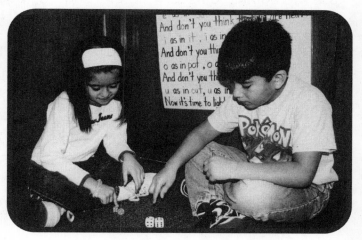

(S) Double Card Addition

Shuffle a deck of cards (with face cards removed) and deal the cards between two players. Both players turn over two cards at a time and announce the sum of the numbers on the cards (with aces being worth one point). The player with the larger sum wins that turn and gets all four cards.

(S) Hidden Counters

Give each pair of children 10 counters. One child takes the counters and puts some in each hand. The partner taps one hand. The child opens that hand, and together the children count the counters. The partner has to figure out how many counters are in the other hand. After he or she answers, both children count the counters in the second hand to check the answer. Partners take turns hiding the counters.

(I) Twenty on the Plate

This game is perfect for individual players. In a game bag, place 20 objects (e.g., math manipulatives, rocks, or seashells), one die, and a small plate. The player puts all the objects on the floor, then rolls the die. He or she then adds that number of objects to the plate. The game is over when all 20 items have been added to the plate.

(I) Domino Addition

Photocopy the Domino Data Sheet (page 25) for each child. Have children select a domino, record the dots on the data sheet, then add the number of dots on both sides of the domino. As children begin to write equations, use the domino dots to write and solve an equation.

(T) Rhyme

As children gather for circle time, recite this rhyme:

Doubles

One and one are two. That I always knew.
Two and two are four. They could be no more.
Three and three are six, whether stones or sticks.
Four and four are eight, if I keep them straight.
Five and five are ten. Let's try it all over again.

T Poem

As children gather for circle time, begin to recite this poem:

The Monkey

One little monkey was looking at you.
He was joined by another and then there were two.
Two little monkeys playing in a tree
Were joined by another and then there were three.
Three little monkeys saw one more,
She came to play with them,
And then there were four.
Four little monkeys happy to be alive,
Were joined by another,
And then there were five.

T Poem

As children gather for circle time, recite this poem:

Over in the Meadow

Over in the meadow, in the sand, in the sun
Lived an old mother frog and her little froggie one.
"Croak!" said the mother. "I croak," said the one.
So they croaked and were happy in the sand, in the sun.

Over in the meadow, in the pond so blue,
Lived an old mother fish and her little fishies two.
"Swim!" said the mother. "We swim," said the two.
So they swam and were happy in the pond so blue.

Over in the meadow, in the nest in the tree,
Lived an old mother bird and her little birdies three.
"Sing!" said the mother. "We sing," said the three.
So they sang and were happy in the nest in the tree.

RA Literacy Links

Fish Eyes: A Book You Can Count On by Lois Ehlert (Harcourt, 1992).
Ehlert features brightly colored fish against the same deep blue background throughout the book. The first few pages feature a number of fish, from 1 to 10, accompanied by a short poem. A recurring dark green fish appears with each set of fish, challenging the reader to add him to the set, thus encouraging the child to add one to each number and predict the number of the next page.

Try This! Have a child (the line leader) go to the door. As he or she stands, the class calls out, "One." That child calls the name of another child and the class calls out, "Two." Repeat this procedure until all children are in line. This activity supports children who are still developing the concept of rationale counting, as well as helping children understand the concept of +1.

One More Bunny: Adding from One to Ten by Rick Walton
(HarperCollins, 2000).
From the creator of So Many Bunnies, this counting book introduces bunnies and other characters, such as bumblebees. The more readers look, the more they will find many different sets of objects and numbers to add.

Try This! Have children create one page of a class book entitled Counting Things in Our Classroom. Remind them to think about the book and have them draw a scene with things to count.

Domino Data Sheet

Draw the dots on your domino here.
Write the number of dots below. Then, add them.

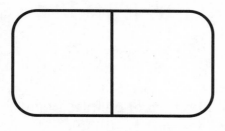

_____ + _____ = _____

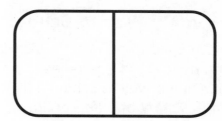

_____ + _____ = _____

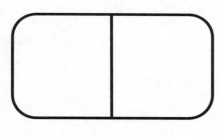

_____ + _____ = _____

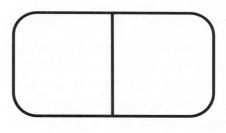

_____ + _____ = _____

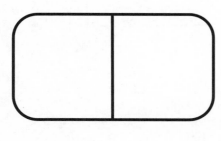

_____ + _____ = _____

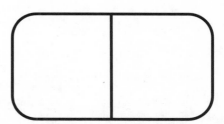

_____ + _____ = _____

SUBTRACTING

W Whole-group activity   **S** Small-group activity

I Individual activity   **T** Transition   **RA** Read-aloud

W On My Way to School

Give each child 10 pennies in a small resealable bag. Tell stories such as: "This morning, I put 5 pennies in my pocket, but there was a hole in my pocket. On the way to school, I lost 2 pennies. How many do I have now?" Repeat this story at different times, changing the numbers of pennies being put into the pocket and getting lost. Using real coins helps keep the children engaged and interested in repeating the activity. (This activity also helps build children's money skills.)

W Missing Ducks

Create five ducks to use as props when chanting "Five Little Ducks" (page 27) and put them in a pocket chart. As the ducks go "over the hill and far away," ask a child to remove all the ducks from the pocket chart. When some of the ducks come back, ask the child to put back the correct number of little ducks in the pocket chart.

Teaching Tip #7
Create mini-books for children by writing the lyrics to "Five Little Ducks," one stanza to a page. Have the children draw the appropriate number of ducks on each page of their mini-book. This way, children can build both reading and math skills at the same time.

(S) Hidden Objects

Give each pair of children a plastic margarine tub with five small similar objects inside (e.g., 1-inch wooden cubes, interlocking cubes, 1-inch tiles, pattern blocks, keys). Have one child hide some of the objects by putting the container upside down over them. Ask the other child to guess how many items are under the container based on the number that's left outside.

(S) Race to Zero

Have children connect 20 interlocking cubes. Ask them to take turns rolling a die and disconnecting the number of cubes shown on the die. The first child who removes all of the cubes wins.

(I) Twenty Off the Plate

In this version of the "Twenty on the Plate" game (page 22), the player puts 20 objects on the plate, rolls a die, then subtracts that number of objects by moving them from the plate onto the floor. The game is over when all 20 items have been subtracted from the plate.

(T) Chant

To get the attention of distracted children, begin chanting:

Five Little Ducks

Five little ducks went out one day
Over the hill and far away.
Mother duck said,
"Quack, quack, quack, quack."
But only four little ducks came back.

Four little ducks went out one day . . .
But only three little ducks came back.

Three little ducks went out one day . . .
But only two little ducks came back.

Two little ducks went out one day . . .
But only one little duck came back.

One little duck went out one day . . .
But none of the five little ducks came back.

Sad mother duck went out one day . . .
The sad mother duck said,
"Quack, quack, quack."
And all of the five little ducks came back.

T Rhyme

As children gather for circle time, recite this rhyme:

Ten in a Bed

There were ten in a bed
And the little one said,
"Roll over, roll over."
So they all rolled over
And one fell out.

There were nine in a bed
And the little one said,
"Roll over, roll over."
So they all rolled over
And one fell out.

There were eight in a bed. . . .

There were seven in a bed. . . .

There were six in a bed. . . .

There were five in a bed. . . .

There were four in a bed. . . .

There were three in a bed. . . .

There were two in a bed
And the little one said,
"Roll over, roll over."
So they all rolled over
And one fell out.

There was one in a bed
And the little one said,
"Good night!"

RA Literacy Link

Five Little Monkeys Jumping on the Bed by Eileen Christelow
(Houghton Mifflin, 1991).
This old rhyme has been made into a book, but the story is the same. As soon as they say good night to their mother, all five monkeys start jumping on the bed. One by one, they fall off the bed and hurt themselves. Children will enjoy the surprise ending.

Try This! Ask groups of five children to dramatize the actions in the book by jumping on a sheet placed on the floor in the middle of a circle of children. Chant the rhyme as they jump and "fall off the bed" back into the circle.

Elevator Magic by Stuart J. Murphy (HarperTrophy, 1997).
Ben and his mom take the elevator down from his mother's office. They make three stops on the way to the ground floor. Each time, Ben uses the elevator buttons as a number line to figure out how many floors down they must go to reach their destination.

Try This! Distribute long strips of paper (cut horizontally from 11- by 17-inch paper). Have children create their own line of elevator buttons. At the next circle time, have children use their elevator buttons to solve subtraction problems, such as, "We are on the 9th floor. What floor will we be on if we go down three floors?"

WHOLES AND PARTS/FRACTIONS

W Whole-group activity   **S** Small-group activity

I Individual activity   **T** Transition   **RA** Read-aloud

W Fraction Puzzles

Use four posterboards of different colors to make fraction puzzles. Cut one posterboard in half, one in thirds, and one in fourths. Put a whole posterboard in the middle of a circle of children. Give the two pieces of posterboard to two children and ask them to complete the "halves" puzzle. Give the three pieces of posterboard to another two children to assemble the "thirds" puzzle, and the four pieces to two more children to finish the "fourths" puzzle. Create smaller puzzles and put them in the math center for children to continue to explore fractions.

W Fractions Words

Write the phrase "Fractions Words" on a posterboard and hang it in the math center. For two or three weeks, spend two minutes before each formal math lesson discussing words that help us talk about parts and wholes: divide, equal, fraction, share, whole, half, third, fourth, part, whole. Each day choose one word, talk about it, write it on an index card, and ask a volunteer to post the card on the Fractions Words poster.

W Half of Half of Half

Give one child a piece of 11- by 17-inch paper. Have the child fold the sheet in half, cut it apart, then hand the other half to another child. Next, have both children fold their sheets in half again, cut them apart, and hand the other halves to other children. Have children continue doing the activity until every child in the class has a piece of paper. Challenge children to figure out what fraction of the original sheet of paper each child got. Are there any leftover pieces of paper?

(S) Sharing Snacks

Have each child share a snack with a partner by dividing the snack into two equal parts. Begin with a snack that can easily be divided into two: bananas, oranges, pears, apples, or an even number of cookies or crackers. Build up to more complex snacks, such as trail mix, snack mix, or dry cereal.

(S) One Half and One Half Equal One

Provide a collection of plastic or wooden rods. Ask children to work together to find two of the same-length rod that, when joined together, equal the length of one long rod. On other days, repeat this same exploration with string, ribbon, and paper strips.

(I) Symmetry Halves

Have children fold a paper in half and paint on one-half of the paper. Have them carefully refold the paper so that the paint covers both sides. Open the paper very carefully and let it dry before posting to show the symmetrical fractions created on the two halves of the paper.

(RA) Literacy Links

Eating Fractions by Bruce McMillan (Scholastic, 1991).
Through photographs of two boys sharing different foods, McMillan demonstrates fractions. First showing the food as a whole (banana, muffin, pizza, corn on the cob, pear salad, and strawberry pie), subsequent photos show the food as it is cut into halves, quarters, and thirds. Recipes are included in the back of the book.

Try This! Have small groups of children decide which fraction they are going to use to divide their snack of bananas and muffins.

The Hershey's Milk Chocolate Bar Fractions Book by Jerry Pallotta and Robert C. Bolster (Cartwheel Books, 1999).
A Hershey's chocolate bar, which is made up of 12 rectangles, lends itself to exploring the concept of fractions. This book leads the reader through each fraction.

Try This! Use Hershey chocolate bars as manipulatives (or same-size rectangles cut from brown card stock) and explore equivalent fractions such as six-twelfths equals one-half, and so on.

INTRODUCTION TO MULTIPLYING/DIVIDING

W Whole-group activity   **S** Small-group activity

I Individual activity   **T** Transition   **RA** Read-aloud

W Finding Equal Groups

Challenge children to identify things that come in a group such as a box of crayons or a pair of gloves. Then find how many of those groups can be found in the classroom. Teachers will need to model this activity until children begin to understand the concept.

Teaching Tip #8

Seeing equal groups in their environment is an early skill necessary for developing an understanding of multiplication. To help children begin to identify equal groups, ask questions such as:
- How many children are wearing two shoes?
- How many children have three cookies for their snack?
- How many tables have four chairs?
- How many chairs have four legs?
- How many hands have five fingers?

S Sharing Equally

Divide the class into small groups. Prepare snacks for each group so that the number of food items is divisible by the number of children in each group (e.g., 32 goldfish crackers for a group of four children or 30 saltine crackers for a group of six children). Challenge the group to divide the snack onto napkins so that everyone in the group gets the same number.

Ⓢ Passing Out Materials

Divide the class into groups of five children. Give one child from each group 15 pieces of paper. Have each group figure out how many pieces of paper each child in the group will get.

ⓇⒶ Literacy Links

The Doorbell Rang by Pat Hutchins (Pearson Learning, 1989).
Ma bakes a dozen cookies for her two children. They divide the cookies between them, but before they begin eating, the doorbell rings. Two neighborhood children have come to play. Now the cookies have to be divided two more ways. The doorbell continues ringing, and the cookies continue to be divided among more people until Grandma saves the day by arriving with her own tray of cookies.

Try This! Distribute large paper towels and resealable bags with 12 cookies in each. During a second read-aloud, have children divide their dozen cookies as new children come into the story.

Stay in Line by Teddy Slater (Scholastic, 1996).
Twelve children take a class trip to the zoo. At first, they line up by 2s, then by 3s, 4s, even by 6s and finally by 12s. Looking at different ways to group 12 introduces children to the concept of arrays, the basic concept of multiplication.

Try This! Have children reenact the grouping and regrouping that the children in the book do.

GEOMETRY

W Whole-group activity **S** Small-group activity

I Individual activity **T** Transition **RA** Read-aloud

W Paper Chains

Show children how to make paper chains by taping strips of paper into circles. Have children make as many chains as they can in three minutes. Place the chains on the floor and tape each child's section together to see how big the group's circle is.

W Geoboards

Provide a geoboard and rubber bands for every child or pair. Encourage children to experiment with making different sized shapes on the geoboard. Discuss why only shapes with straight lines can be made on geoboards.

Teaching Tip #9
After children have played with geoboards, put several geoboards in the math center for further exploration. Challenge children to draw the shapes they create using the geoboard reproducible on page 38.

(W) Geometry Words

Write the phrase "Geometry Words" on a posterboard and hang it in the math center. For two or three weeks, spend two minutes before each formal math lesson discussing words that help us talk about geometry: sides, corners, circle, oval, square, rectangle, triangle, hexagon, rhombus, parallelogram, cube, cylinder, cone, sphere. Each day choose one word, talk about it, write it on an index card, and ask a volunteer to post the card on the Geometry Words poster.

(S) Class Book of Shapes

Encourage children to work in small groups to find circles, squares, and rectangles in the classroom. If possible, allow children to photograph them, then use the photographs to create a class-made book. You can extend this activity by taking a walking field trip around the school to look for circles, squares, and rectangles (plus other shapes) in the children's environment.

(S) Shapes Concentration

Make Concentration cards by drawing triangles, squares, rectangles, circles, ovals, and any other shapes the class is learning on index cards. Put one shape on each card, and create two cards per shape. Show the class how to play Concentration by starting with all the cards placed face down. One person turns over two cards. If the cards have the same shape, that player gets to keep both cards. If not, the cards are turned face down again, and the next player turns over two cards. The game is over when all the matches have been made.

(I) Shape Paintings

Cut paper into large shapes on which children can paint. There's no rule that says all paintings have to be created on rectangle paper—offer children large circles, ovals, squares, or triangles on which to paint. Reinforce the correct vocabulary as children choose the shapes for their "canvas."

Teaching Tip #10
Instead of buying commercially produced shapes to hang on classroom walls or on a bulletin board, hang the children's shape paintings to help them learn to name shapes. Children are much more inclined to remember information when it's meaningful to them.

❶ Shape Collage

Make several copies of the different shapes on page 39 on different colored card stock and cut them out. Provide a die, a shape spinner (page 39), scissors, gluestick, and card stock. Have children roll the die and spin the spinner to determine how many of which shapes to use to create their picture.

Teaching Tip #11

Ask parent volunteers to cut out shapes for the Shape Collage activity if children's fine motor skills are not developed well enough to use scissors with ease.

❶ Build a Shape

Provide straws, gumdrops, and drawings of shapes with straight sides. Invite children to make triangles, squares, and rectangles by connecting the straws with the gumdrops. (You can use play dough in place of gumdrops).

❶ Cover the Card

Distribute task cards (these can be purchased commercially or created by the teacher) and pattern blocks to partners. Have children explore different ways to fill the outline drawings using the pattern blocks.

❶ Crazy Quilts

Have children cut out 20 to 30 geometric shapes with straight sides, then piece them together to create a quilt piece. Gluing the shapes on graph paper may help children keep the sides of their quilt piece straight.

Teaching Tip #12

If you have access to a crazy quilt, bring it into the classroom to share with children. If you can't find one, try to find a photograph in a book or on the Internet.

RA Literacy Links

Not Enough Room! by Joanne Rocklin (Scholastic, 1998).
Two sisters each have their own square room until a new baby comes into the family. Now, they have to share one room. They try dividing it several different ways, but Mom is the one who comes up with the best idea: buy bunk beds and share the whole room.

Try This! Have small groups of children work together to measure tables or bookshelves, and have them attach tape to divide the furniture in half.

A Cloak for the Dreamer by Aileen Friedman (Scholastic, 1995).
A tailor's three sons are given the task of creating a cloak for the Archduke. The first son creates his from rectangles. The second son creates two cloaks, one from squares and one from triangles. The third son creates his cloak from circles. Obviously, that cloak has holes in it and cannot be given to the Archduke. The father and the first two sons stay up all night cutting the circles into hexagons and sewing a cloak for the third son. The watercolor paintings feature the geometric shapes used to create the cloaks.

Try This! Use the four shapes in this book (die-cut shapes) for children to create and recreate patterns.

Geoboard Sheet

Draw the shapes you made on your geoboard here.

FUN-FILLED 5-TO-10-MINUTE MATH ACTIVITIES FOR YOUNG LEARNERS

Shape Collage

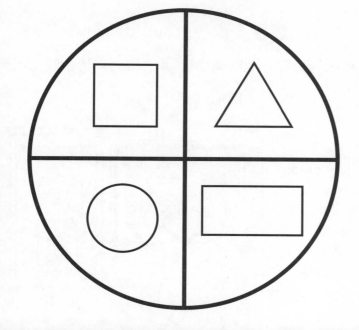

Spinner

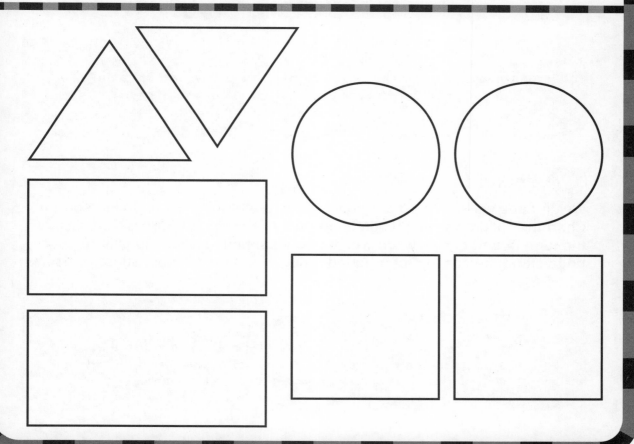

MEASURING

W Whole-group activity **S** Small-group activity

I Individual activity **T** Transition **RA** Read-aloud

W Step by Step

Have children estimate how many steps it takes to go from the classroom's meeting area to the door. By walking heel-to-toe, children can count their steps and compare their estimates to the real count.

Teaching Tip #13
As a variation to the "Step by Step" activity, trace a child's foot onto card stock and cut out several footprints for children to use in measuring length.

W Pound for Pound

Weigh three children on a bathroom scale (preferably with a digital read-out). Chart the children's weights on chart paper or a posterboard. Then discuss the term pound and how we weigh people in pounds. To help children understand the concept of a pound, bring in a pound bag of sugar or flour.

Teaching Tip #14
After the "Pound for Pound" activity, place the chart and the scale in the math center and encourage other children to weigh themselves and chart their weight.

(W) Measuring Words

Write the phrase "Measuring Words" on a posterboard and hang it in the math center. For two or three weeks, spend two minutes before each formal math lesson discussing words that help us talk about measurement: short, long, inch, centimeter, foot, ruler, measuring tape. Each day choose one word, define it, talk about it, write it on an index card, and ask one child to put the card on the Measuring Words poster.

(S) Exploring Measurement in the Water Center

Encourage children to explore measuring liquids by working in the water center with a variety of measuring cups and measuring spoons. Challenge children to figure out measuring problems, such as, "How many 1/4 cups are needed to make a cup, a pint, or a quart?"

(S) How Long Is the Table?

Divide the class into groups of five children, and have them gather around tables of the same length. Have each group use different nonstandard units of measurement to determine their table's length (e.g., using paper clips, linking chains, interlocking cubes, or any other items in the classroom). Bring the groups back to the meeting area and record their results. This activity can be repeated measuring any other object in the class (e.g., desks of the same size, books of the same height, or bookshelves of the same length).

(S) Balancing Play Dough

Provide a small group of children with a balance scale, three or four weights (in ounces and grams), and play dough. Have children place a weight on one side of the scale, then challenge them to put the exact amount of play dough on the other side to equal the weight. Have the group take the lump of play dough, record its weight on a card, and place the card beside the lump. Repeat for the other weights.

(S) Measure a Friend

Have children work in partners to measure each other's height using interlocking cubes. Chart the children's heights. In another measuring session, have partners measure the length of legs, arms, feet, or other body parts.

I Paper People

As an extension to "Measure a Friend," have children trace each other onto very large butcher paper. Invite children to color or paint facial features and clothes on their paper bodies, then measure different body parts. They can then record and compare their measurements.

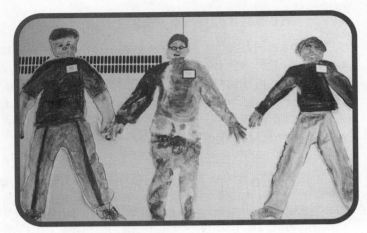

I Light, Heavy, Heavier

Fill three one-pound coffee cans (or other similar containers) with three different materials, such as cotton balls, sand, and water. Challenge children to put the cans in order from lightest to heaviest. Encourage the children to explain why the same-size container can weigh different amounts. To help children connect words to concepts, trace three cans on a posterboard, label each circle with a word ("Light," "Heavy," "Heavier"), and encourage children to place cans in the correct circle.

I Play-Dough Snakes

Provide each child with a standard ruler and play dough. Challenge children to roll out the play dough to make a snake exactly 12 inches long (or any other length that children can easily see by using an inch ruler, a centimeter ruler, or a specified length of yarn or string). Display the snakes on a poster-board labeled with the measurement "Exactly 12 Inches." Then challenge children to create snakes that are less than 12 inches and more than 12 inches. Sort those on two other posterboards labeled "Less Than 12 Inches" and "More than 12 Inches."

I Paper-Clip Measurement

Ask children to connect paper clips and use them to measure the height and width of a book. Ask them to record their answers and compare measurements at the next group meeting.

(T) Song

As children get ready to leave circle time to measure things, sing:

Measuring

(sung to the tune of "The Addams Family")

Refrain:
Da-da-da-dah (snap, snap)
Da-da-da-dah (snap, snap)
Da-da-da-dah
Da-da-da-dah
Da-da-da-dah (snap, snap)

Verse:
I'm going to measure now.
I think I do know how.
I'm really going to wow
My teacher and my friends.

(RA) Literacy Links

How Big is a Foot? by Rolf Myller and Susan McCrath (Young Yearling, 1991).
The King wants to give the Queen a bed for her birthday, but there is a problem. Beds have not been invented yet, so no one knows how long or wide to make a bed. How can the workers figure out how big to make the bed?

Try This! Ask children to measure their beds at home and bring the measurements to class. Then ask them to "draw" their beds on the floor using string the same length as their beds.

Pigs Go to the Market: Fun with Math and Shopping by Amy Axelrod (Aladdin Books, 1999).
Grandma and Grandpa Pig agree to help with the Pig family's Halloween party. Instead of helping get ready for the party, they eat all the Halloween candy. The Pig family races to the grocery store where Mrs. Pig wins a 5-minute shopping spree. The candy aisle covers a two-page spread, complete with weights listed in both ounces and grams.

Try This! Have children bring in one item from the grocery store that lists its weight in both ounces and grams. Have children compare their items and put them in order from lightest to heaviest.

ESTIMATING

W Whole-group activity   **S** Small-group activity

I Individual activity   **T** Transition   **RA** Read-aloud

S Spoon Lengths

Divide the class into small groups. Give each group a spoon to hold and inspect. Then, have children leave the spoon on their table and search the room for objects that are about the same length as the spoon. Have children take their items back to the table and compare them to the spoon to see which one most closely matches the spoon's length.

Teaching Tip #15

Young children need many measuring experiences before they realize the importance of lining up objects to be measured at the same baseline. Show children how to place the bottom of each item on a line and compare the lengths of items. Remind children about this each time they measure objects until they can remember on their own.

S Packing Peanuts

Replace sand in the sand center with packing peanuts. Give each group of children a small box. Challenge them to put 20 packing peanuts in the box without actually counting the peanuts. After children finish their estimation, invite them to count the peanuts to see how close they got to 20.

Teaching Tip #16

The "Packing Peanuts" activity can be done with any number. It would be best to begin this activity with a smaller number and build to 100 over a period of several days.

S Parking Lot Estimation

Ask several small groups of children to estimate how many cars are in the school's parking lot. (For safety reasons, this activity is best done if the parking lot can be viewed from the school's playground.) Have another group of children count the actual number of cars. Then compare the estimates to the actual count. Try this activity again at different times of the day on different days, when more or fewer cars tend to be parked in the lot.

I Estimating Length

Give children a length of yarn. Ask them to estimate how many paper clips it would take to match the yarn. Have children record their estimates, place paper clips in a line beside the yarn, count them, and record the actual count.

Teaching Tip #17
Extend the "Estimating Length" activity by substituting interlocking cubes for the paper clips. Some children may notice that the cubes are smaller than the paper clips and adjust their estimate accordingly.

I Estimation Jar

Place a jar approximately half-filled with marbles near the entrance to the classroom. Put small slips of paper and several pencils nearby. As children come into the classroom in the morning, ask them to estimate and record how many marbles they think are in the jar. At circle time, count the marbles to see whose estimate came closest to the real number. Let the children see you remove several marbles from the jar, but don't let them know how many. Remind children that their estimate tomorrow should be less than the actual count from today because some marbles were taken away. Repeat this activity for several days until most of the children are making more educated estimates based on whether you add or remove marbles in the jar.

ⓘ Pegs for Pegboards

Have a child take handfuls of pegs from a large container of pegs until he or she thinks there's enough to fill an entire pegboard. Then, ask the child to put the pegs into each hole to determine if he or she chose too few, too many, or just enough pegs.

Teaching Tip #18
To extend the "Pegs for Pegboards" activity, have a child roll a die or spin a number spinner and put pegs into the board according to the numbers generated by the die or spinner. This activity reinforces counting and one-to-one correspondence skills.

ⓘ Estimating Tiles

Give each child a 2-foot length of yarn and ask him or her to form a square or rectangle with the yarn. Then, challenge the child to estimate the number of 1-inch tiles it would take to fill the shape. Have him or her record the estimate, fill in the shape, count those tiles, and record the actual count.

RA Literacy Link

Betcha! by Stuart J. Murphy (HarperCollins, 1997).
Two friends read about a contest, in which the person who gets closest to the number of jellybeans in the jar wins two tickets to the All-Star Game. On their way to the toy store where the contest is being held, they estimate other things—the number of people on the bus, the number of cars in a traffic jam, the total prices of goods in a window. Each time they use a different strategy to estimate. At the toy store, one of the friends wins the contest and shares the tickets with the other.

Try This! Recreate the jellybean estimation contest. Put a small jar filled with jellybeans in the math center, along with small slips of paper for children to record their estimates and initials. During the next circle time, count the jellybeans together and determine who guessed the closest number.

TIME

W Whole-group activity   **S** Small-group activity

I Individual activity   **T** Transition   **RA** Read-aloud

W Daily Schedule

Present the daily schedule listed as a simple order of daily events: circle time, shared reading, writing workshop, center time, and so on. To help emergent readers read the schedule, include rebus pictures. As children develop reading skills and the ability to tell time, you can include the actual time for each activity.

W A Minute of Activity

Help one or more children operate a stopwatch to determine just how long a minute is. Have the other children engage in a predetermined activity during that one minute (e.g., stand on one foot, jump up and down in place, or do jumping jacks).

S About a Minute

As a follow-up to "A Minute of Activity," ask children to brainstorm a list of things they do every day that they think would take about a minute to do (e.g., put on socks and shoes, tie their shoes, button a shirt, or eat a banana). Pair up children, and have one child do one of the activities listed and the other use a stopwatch to time him or her. How long did the activity take to complete?

W Time Words

Write the phrase "Time Words" on a posterboard and hang it in the math center. For two or three weeks, spend two minutes before each formal math lesson discussing words that help us talk about time: morning, afternoon, evening, night, today, tomorrow, yesterday, date, week, days of the week, year, months of the year, calendar, minute, second, hour, clock, watch. Each day choose one word, talk about it, write it on an index card, and ask a child to post the card on the Time Words poster.

S Times of Our Lives

Set the correct time on a toy clock with movable hands. In a group of four to six children, have the children set individual clocks to the same time. Set the clock to different times that are meaningful to children—the time school starts, lunchtime, recess time, the time the end-of-the-day bell rings. Invite children to reset their own clocks each time.

W Paper-Plate Clocks

As an extention to "Times of Our Lives," make paper-plate clocks that show important times of the school day. Post the clocks in a prominent place near the classroom clock so children can compare the real clock with times that are important to the class.

School Starts | Center Time | Lunch Time | Recess! | End of Day

I Beat the Clock

Show children how to set a kitchen timer for two minutes, then put the timer and recording sheets in the math center. On one day, challenge children to see how many times they can bounce a ball in two minutes. Ask them to record their numbers on the recording sheets. On another day, challenge them to see how many coins they can put into a piggy bank in two minutes. Each day, change the activity.

T Five-Minute Warning Timer

Give a 5-minute warning to help children with the transition from center time to cleaning up. Set a kitchen timer to five minutes to help children develop a sense of how long five minutes is—and so that the 5-minute warning is truly five minutes.

T Rhyme

As children gather for circle time, recite this rhyme:

The Clock

With a tick and a tock,
And a tick and a tock,
The clock goes round all day.
It tell us when it's time to work
And when it's time to play.

(T) Rhyme

Here's another rhyme for transition time:

I Like You

I like you in the morning
And in the afternoon.
I like you in the evening
Underneath the moon.

I like you when we eat breakfast
And when we eat our lunch.
I like you when we eat dinner.
I like you quite a bunch.

(RA) Literacy Links

The Grouchy Ladybug by Eric Carle (HarperCollins, 1996).
Every hour, on the hour, a grouchy ladybug challenges an increasingly larger animal. "Hey, you wanna fight?" is the repeating phrase. The animals all turn her down—until she encounters a large whale.

Try This! Stop whatever the class is doing at the top of the hour. Ask the children to return to the meeting area and quickly create a page for a class book. Use sentences such as, "At 8:00, we were reading poetry," "At 9:00, we were working in centers," or "At 10:00, we were writing our own stories."

Just a Minute by Teddy Slater (Scholastic, 1996).
Fred wants to show his new drawing to his family, but everyone he approaches says, "Just a minute."

Try This! Use a stopwatch to find out whether or not the author is correct about the fact that counting to "60 Mississippi" takes one minute. Lead the class in counting, "one Mississippi, two Mississippi, three Mississippi, four Mississippi, five Mississippi," and so on until you reach one minute on the stopwatch. How far did you get?

MONEY

W Whole-group activity   **S** Small-group activity

I Individual activity   **T** Transition   **RA** Read-aloud

W Money Words

Write the phrase "Money Words" on a posterboard and hang it in the math center. For two or three weeks, spend two minutes before each formal math lesson discussing words that help us talk about money: penny, nickel, dime, quarter, half dollar, dollar bill. Each day choose one word, talk about it, write it on an index card, and ask a child to post the card on the Money Words poster.

S Circle Time Shopping

Give every child in a small group a certain amount of money, such as 10 cents. In the middle of the circle of children, place three cafeteria trays of differently priced items the children can purchase, such as pieces of candy for 1 cent each, animal-shaped erasers for 3 cents each, and sparkly pencils for 7 cents each. Children can buy any group of items that equal 10 cents or they can save their dime to buy a cookie in the cafeteria. As children make their purchasing decisions, ask them to explain why they are deciding what to buy.

S Coins From Around the World

After children can consistently recognize U.S. coins, introduce them to a collection of international coins (collected from banks, family members who travel, or friends who live outside the U.S.). Give partners 10 to 12 different coins in a small resealable bag and ask them to sort the coins according to their own rules. Invite kids to share their rules of sorting.

S Race to 25

Teach children how to play "Race to 25." Place 25 pennies, five nickels, two dimes, one die, and one small plate in a resealable bag. To play the game, a player rolls the die and adds that number of pennies to his or her plate. When the player accumulates five pennies, he or she can exchange them for one nickel; two nickels can be exchanged for one dime, and so on.

Ⓘ Grocery-Store Clerk

Bring in 10 items from the grocery store with prices clearly marked on the top of the can or box. Place the items in the dramatic play center, and ask children, one at a time, to enter the prices into a calculator (or, if possible, an adding machine with running tape) and write the total on an index card.

Ⓘ Careful Shopper

Put grocery circulars, calculators, and lined paper for grocery lists in the math center. Challenge children to use the circulars to write a list of items they can purchase for under $1.00. Increase the dollar amount as children become more accomplished with this activity.

ⓇⒶ Literacy Links

Pigs Will be Pigs: Fun With Math and Money by Amy Axelrod (Aladdin, 1997). When the Pig family decides to go out to eat, Mr. Pig discovers he has only $1 in his wallet. The family hunts throughout their house to find enough money to pay for their dinners. They finally find enough to order the specials from their favorite Mexican food restaurant (menu included in the book).

Try This! Organize a money hunt within the classroom. Just as the Pig family hunted for money to buy dinner, children could hunt for money to purchase food, such as ice cream for dessert at lunch.

Penny Pot: Counting Coins by Stuart J. Murphy (HarperTrophy, 1998). Jessie and her friends learn about different ways to make fifty cents when they spend their time at a face-painting booth. The story offers different opportunities to practice counting coins.

Try This! Give each child a small baggie with several coins. During a second read-aloud, encourage children to group some of their coins in the same way that children in the story do.

Try This, Too! Teach children who have become experts at playing "Race to 25" how to play "Race to 50." Place 50 pennies, 10 nickels, five dimes, two quarters, one die, and a small plate in a resealable bag. Put two or three game bags in the math center. The same rules apply: When a player accumulates five pennies, they can be exchanged for one nickel, two nickels can be exchanged for one dime, and so on.

GRAPHING

W Whole-group activity   S Small-group activity

I Individual activity   T Transition   RA Read-aloud

W Shower-Curtain Graphs

Buy an inexpensive plastic shower curtain and draw a large grid on it with a permanent marker. Use the grid as a large floor graph. Every day for a week, label the bottom row of the grid with different attributes, such as hair color, eye color, shirt color, or type of shoes. Invite children to graph themselves by standing on the correct column according to the attribute of the day.

Teaching Tip #19

Graphing is a difficult concept for many young children. Initially, choose topics that are of high interest to children, such as favorite snacks or pets, and make the graphs concrete. Wait until children have had many experiences with graphing before asking them to complete a graph on paper.

W How Many Siblings?

On a posterboard, create a graph with as many columns as the number of siblings that children in the class have. Ask children to draw a picture of each of their brothers and sisters and post the picture in the correct column.

W Graphing Shoes

Divide a posterboard into four columns and label the columns "buckles," "shoelaces," "Velcro," and "no fasteners." Give each child a sticky note. Ask children to write their names on the notes and place them on the correct column, depending on the type of fastener on their shoes. You can repeat this graph at various times and compare the different results.

W Voting for Read-Aloud

Place two books on the chalkboard shelf and draw a line on the board between the two books. Ask children to vote for the book they would like to hear read aloud at the end of center time by writing their names above the book they prefer.

> **Teaching Tip #20**
> Another way to record votes is to have children write their names on sticky notes, then place them in the appropriate column. When time is a factor, this way is quicker than waiting for each child to write his or her name on the chart.

W Voting for Favorite Book of the Week

At the end of each week, make reduced photocopies of the front covers of five books you've read to the class. Divide a posterboard into five columns and attach a photocopied book cover to the bottom of each column. Invite children to vote for the book that they liked most. They can write their names on self-adhesive labels or draw their favorite part of the book on sticky notes and place them on the correct column.

Our Favorite Books!

	The Very Hungry Caterpillar	10 Black Dots	Swimmy	Snowy Day	Curious George
8					
7			Kelli		
6			Rosa		
5			Josue		
4	Jamie		Caleb	Mela	
3	Jorge		Maria	Zachary	Theo
2	Kim	Tam	Kama	Jeremy	Liza
1	Lakwan	Norma	Sarah	Dash	Debbie

S Ice-Cube Tray Graphing

An ice-cube tray can serve as a 3-dimensional graph. Offer two types of small objects (e.g., coins or candies) for children to sort, count, and place into the sections of an ice-cube tray. After children have had lots of experience with ice-cube tray graphing, challenge them to transfer their data to a chart on paper.

I Recording Dice Rolls

Prepare a grid on an 8 1/2- by 11-inch paper with 6 squares across and 5 down. Label the bottom row with the numbers 1 through 6. Give a student the recording sheet, a die, and pencil. Show him or her how to roll the die, count the dots, and record the roll by entering the number in the square above the preprinted number. (This will also help reinforce the idea that graphs are completed from the bottom of the page up.)

> ### Teaching Tip #21
> For a simpler game, create dice that have only the numbers 1, 2, and 3 on them. Use blank cubes and a permanent marker to create these dice.

I Graphing Snacks

Prepare snacks with three different small items (e.g., goldfish crackers, teddy-bear crackers, and small pretzels) in small resealable bags. Photocopy the 1-inch graph paper (page 56) for each child. Invite children to sort their snacks and place similar items in their own columns on the graph. As they eat each item, have them draw a small representation of that snack on the graph. This way, children have a record of the bags' contents even after they have eaten their snacks.

I Collecting and Graphing Data

Ask each child to think about a question that requires two alternatives for the answer. For example, "What is your favorite fruit—apple or banana?" or "Which would you rather have for breakfast—toast or cereal?" Encourage children to poll their classmates and keep track of answers using tally marks. Then help them complete a two-column graph showing their data.

① Graphing Candies

Have children count out 20 colored candies (such as Skittles or M&M's), then graph them on 1-inch graph paper (page 56). Some children may still need to place the candies on the graph paper to help them color in the squares. Other children will be able to count the number of candies of each color and simply color in the squares.

RA Literacy Link

The Best Vacation Ever by Stuart Murphy (HarperTrophy, 1997). A family cannot agree about where to go on vacation, so the daughter collects data and creates charts to help make this decision. The story of using math to solve this family problem is told through simple rhyming text.

Try This! Have children brainstorm a list of possible sites for a field trip. Write the field-trip sites on a chart and have children vote on their favorite destination. If making this type of decision is not feasible in your school, have children collect data about a favorite place to go with their mom or dad on a weekend.

One-Inch Graph Paper

PATTERNING

W Whole-group activity   **S** Small-group activity

I Individual activity   **T** Transition   **RA** Read-aloud

W Even-Odd Calendar Patterns

Write the numbers for dates on two different shapes—odd numbers on one shape, even numbers on another. (You can also use two sticky notes of different colors.) Every day, invite a child to post the date on a blank calendar grid. A minute of discussion with the class about the calendar will reinforce the concept of the ABAB pattern, as well as the concept of even and odd numbers. As children develop a better sense of the ABAB pattern, introduce more complicated patterns.

W Lining Up

Make patterning the focus of lining up to give children something else to think about instead of trying to be first in line. The most obvious pattern is boy/girl, but you can offer dozens of variations: shirt/sweater, face forward/face backward, hands in the air/hands out to the side, feet together/feet apart, and so on. Invite children to chant the pattern before leaving the classroom.

S Sentence-Strip Patterns

Give partners a sentence strip and two markers of different colors. Ask each child to decide on one shape or picture he or she wants to draw. Have the partners take turns drawing their shape or picture to create an ABAB pattern. Display each pair's sentence-strip patterns on the wall near the math center.

(S) Eating Utensils Patterns

Set up the dramatic-play center as a home or a restaurant. Ask the children playing there to put all the silverware on a table and create an ABCABC pattern with the knives, forks, and spoons.

(I) Interlocking-Cube Trains

Use interlocking cubes to snap together a model pattern for children to copy and extend. When children are at the beginning stage of understanding patterns, provide a simple model (e.g., blue-green-blue-green). As children become more sophisticated in their patterning abilities, you can give them a more complex model to follow (e.g. blue-green-green-red-white-white-blue-green-green-red-white-white.)

(I) Stringing Beads

Give children two different colored beads and a shoestring, tied in a knot on one end. Work with children to string the first few beads in an ABAB pattern, then let them continue working on their own. As children gain confidence and competency, demonstrate more complex patterns (e.g., ABCABC, AABAAB, AABBCCAABBCC) and ask children to recreate these patterns.

(I) Fruit Kabobs

Provide small wooden skewers and a selection of three different fruits, such as grapes, strawberries, and banana slices. Invite children to make ABCABC patterns with the fruits before eating their snacks.

(I) Patterning Stamps

Provide a collection of rubber stamps, ink pads, and rolls of adding-machine paper. Encourage children to use the stamps to make really long patterns over a number of days.

(T) Clapping Patterns

Catch children's attention by starting a clapping pattern and signaling the children to join in (e.g. clap–snap–clap–snap or clap hands 1, 2... 1,2,3...1,2...1,2,3). Over time, make the clapping patterns as complex as the class can understand and mimic.

(T) Chant

As children gather for circle time, begin to recite this rhyme:

Miss Mary Mack

Miss Mary Mack, Mack, Mack,
All dressed in black, black, black,
With silver buttons, buttons, buttons,
All down her back, back, back.

She asked her mother, mother, mother,
For fifty cents, cents, cents,
To see the elephant, elephant, elephant,
Jump the fence, fence, fence.

He jumped so high, high, high,
He reached the sky, sky, sky,
And didn't come back, back, back,
'Til the fourth of July, July, July.

He fell so fast, fast, fast,
He fell so hard, hard, hard,
He made a hole, hole, hole,
In her back yard, yard, yard.

T **Chant**

As children gather for circle time, begin to recite this rhyme:

Boys and Girls in Our Class

Boy, girl, boy, girl, boy, girl, girl
Boy, girl, boy, girl, boy, girl, girl
Jonathan, Janet, Jonathan, Janet, Jonathan, Janet, Janet
Jonathan, Janet, Jonathan, Janet, Jonathan, Janet, Janet

Substitute names of children in the class and repeat using several different names.

RA **Literacy Links**

Beep, Beep, Vroom, Vroom! by Stuart J. Murphy (HarperCollins, 1999).
When Kevin leaves the room, his younger sister, Molly, plays with his cars.
He has told her not to touch his cars, and even lined up his red, blue, and
yellow cars in a special pattern so he will know if they've been moved.
Whenever anyone walks into the room, Molly lines up the cars, using a
different pattern each time. When Kevin walks back into the room, however,
the cars are in the exact same order as he had left them.

Try This! Give each child a resealable bag with four red, four blue, and four
yellow 1-inch squares. As you reread the story, use the squares to represent
the cars that Molly plays with and rearranges into different patterns. Pause
in reading the story after each pattern and help children read the pattern
they've created.

Mouse Views: What the Class Pet Saw by Bruce McMillan (Holiday House, 1994).
McMillan follows a class pet as it explores the school, taking double photographs at several points during the mouse's journey. The first photograph
is shot very close, from the pet's point of view; the second is shot from a
person's point of view. The photos nicely illustrate the intriguing patterns
that can be found in everyday things.

Try This! Challenge children to work in pairs and spy patterns on objects in
the classroom. Provide magnifying glasses for each pair to add an element
of detective work to the activity.

SORTING AND CLASSIFYING

W Whole-group activity   **S** Small-group activity

I Individual activity   **T** Transition   **RA** Read-aloud

W Matching Colors

Place a red posterboard in the middle of a circle of children. Ask them to look around the room for any object that's the same color as the poster-board. After a minute or so, ask children to get their red object and place it on the posterboard. Repeat this activity as often as needed until children can recognize the color red. Then extend the activity using other colors. (Before doing this activity with a class, ensure that many objects of the color you're teaching can easily be seen from the meeting area—e.g., pattern blocks, crayons, markers, construction paper, books, and so on.)

W Guess My Sorting Rule

Put together a collection of items that can be sorted into two distinct groups in a resealable bag (see the list below). You can fill up any extra five minutes with a "Guess My Sorting Rule" activity. Take items out of the bag one at a time and place them in two different groups. Challenge children to guess the sorting rule as you sort the items. Some of the bags could include:

- pencil, marker, colored pencil, crayon, highlighter, index card, sticky note pad, plain white paper, paper stock (things to write with and things to write on)

- pattern block, interlocking cube, linking chain, bolt, nut, nail, key (things that are plastic and things that are metal)

(W) Clean Up, Clean Up

In an organized classroom, everything has its place, and cleaning up is a natural sorting activity. Encourage children to work together to put everything in the classroom back where it belongs. To create a "sorting" environment, try these:

- Draw an outline of block shapes on the shelves of the block center.

- Draw an outline of water-center materials on a pegboard.

- Place word and picture clues on shelves (e.g., write "Pattern Blocks" and draw a picture of pattern blocks on the math shelf).

- Label baskets or containers of books (e.g., Eric Carle books, counting books, poetry books).

(W) Sorting Friends

Use plastic hula-hoops to encourage children to sort themselves. Invite children to sort themselves by one characteristic: a color they are wearing, the type of shoes they are wearing, the color of their hair, and so on.

(S) Sorting Seashells

Ask a small group of children to sort a collection of seashells. Encourage children to decide on their own how to sort the seashells. Listening to the conversation among children as they sort will give you good insight into how different children understand the concept of sorting and classifying.

(S) Stocking the Writing Center

Assign the task of restocking writing center materials to a small group of children who need additional experience with sorting. Ask them to sort new paper by color and add the paper to the correct container, add markers to the marker containers, and crayons to the crayon containers. This will help reinforce what they know about sorting.

S Playing Librarian

Ask children to work together to sort new books into pre-established reading-center baskets and containers.

Teaching Tip #22
Before children can sort books by themselves, they need to observe you putting away books according to a system. Try organizing children's books into categories such as alphabet books, counting books, books about animals, books about families, and author-of-the-week books.

I Snacks

Serve a snack mix that has been put into individual resealable bags. Give each child a bag of snack mix and a plate. Encourage children to sort their snack before eating.

I Sorting Keys

Gather a collection of 20 to 25 keys. Ask each child to sort the keys by any attribute he or she chooses.

Teaching Tip #23
Photograph each child and the way he or she sorted the keys. Post the photographs on a bulletin board and lead a class discussion about how different children sorted the keys in different ways.

RA Literacy Links

The Button Box by Margarette S. Reid (Penguin Putnam, 1995).
This simple little book shares the experience of a boy and his grandmother as they sort through the grandmother's collection of buttons.

Try This! Give each child in the class 10 to 12 buttons in a small resealable bag. (For the first few times, make sure that every child has the same set of buttons.) Ask the children to sort the buttons by a particular attribute (e.g., color, size, shape, or number of holes). After children have had multiple experiences sorting buttons, you can vary the number or type of buttons in each bag and let children choose their own sorting attributes.

Try This, Too! Put a collection of buttons in the math center. Encourage a child who is struggling with the concept of sorting to find all the red buttons or all the buttons with one hole. Invite children who are comfortable sorting by one or two attributes to choose their own sorting rules.

More or Less a Mess by Sheila Keenan (Scholastic, 1997).
Told in rhyming phrases, this is the story of a little girl overwhelmed by the task of cleaning her room. First, she sorts her things by color, then by how she uses them, and then by where they belong. But when she hears her mother coming up the stairs, she hides everything under her bed covers.

Try This! Read this story right before a major clean-up time (i.e., at the end of the week). Talk about sorting items in the classroom and working together to put all items where they belong.